The Kids' Book of
Secret Codes, Signals, and Ciphers

The Kids' Book of

Secret Codes, Signals, and Ciphers

E. A. Grant

RUNNING PRESS
Philadelphia, Pennsylvania

Canadian representatives: General Publishing Co., Ltd., 30 Lesmill Road, Don Mills, Ontario M3B 2T6.

International representatives: Worldwide Media Services, Inc., 115 East Twenty-third Street, New York, New York 10010.

9   8   7   6   5   4   3   2

Digit on the right indicates the number of this printing.

Library of Congress Cataloging-in-Publication Data
Grant, E.A.
    The kids' book of secret codes, signals & ciphers / E.A. Grant. p. cm.
    Summary: Discusses the history and different varieties of codes and ciphers, describing code machines, signals, sign language, picture languages, and hidden messages.
    ISBN 0–89471–781–2 : $6.95
    1. Cryptography—Juvenile literature. 2. Ciphers—Juvenile literature. [1. Cryptography. 2. Ciphers.] I. Title.
Z103.3.G7 1989   89–43029
652'.8—dc20   CIP
                                                              AC

ISBN 0–89471–781–2

Cover design by Toby Schmidt
Interior design by Linda Jovinelly Franklin
Cover photographs by Will Brown
Photo of Eleanor A. Grant by Brian West
Semaphore Alphabet on pages 44–45 courtesy of Boy Scouts of America. Rosetta Stone on page 55 reproduced by courtesy of the Trustees of the British Museum.
Illustrations on pages 3, 5, 6, 7, 9, 13, 19, 24, 33, 35, 37, 41, 48, 49, 51, 53, 58, 61, and 71 by Len Epstein; illustrations on pages 14, 32, 39, 54, 56, 57, 58, 59, 65, 66, 67, and 77 by E. Michael Epps; illustrations on pages 45, 76, and 78 by Lisa Lentz.

Typography by Commcor Communications Corporation, Philadelphia, Pennsylvania
Printed by The Collett Company, Victor, New York

This book may be ordered by mail from the publisher. Please add $2.50 for postage and handling for each copy. *But try your bookstore first!*

Running Press Book Publishers
125 South Twenty-second Street
Philadelphia, Pennsylvania 19103

Contents

The Science of Secrets

In a faraway land, many years ago, two queens ruled two neighboring countries. The queens, Mary and Elizabeth, were cousins, and each felt that she alone should rule both countries. Elizabeth, the more powerful of the two, arranged for Mary to be captured and imprisoned in a castle for many years. But Mary continued to hope that some day she would escape and defeat her cousin. She wrote messages in code to her friends, and had her servants smuggle them out of the castle in the hollowed-out corks of barrels of beer.

Mary didn't know that Elizabeth's soldiers knew about the messages. One who was particularly clever at codes figured out what the messages meant. He warned Elizabeth of Mary's plots, and poor Mary was beheaded.

What may sound like a dark and dangerous fairy tale really happened, about 400 years ago. The cousins were Mary, Queen of Scots, and Elizabeth I, Queen of England.

Throughout history, stories like this one have unfolded, and the fates of many people have been shaped by the making and breaking of secret codes.

Because keeping secrets—and trying to figure out the secrets of others—is so important, a whole science has grown around it. This science is called cryptology (krip-TAHL-uh-jee), which means "secret word" in Greek. All around the world, thousands of cryptologists try to make unbreakable secret codes and work at figuring out how to read other people's codes. Presidents and kings make hard decisions based on what cryptologists tell them.

But presidents and kings aren't the only ones who have secrets to keep and messages to send—you and I do, too! Luckily for us, the science of keeping secrets isn't always difficult and mysterious.

It's also fun and easy, once you know how. That's what this book is all about.

You can make secret messages in two ways. First, you can hide the message—by using invisible ink, for example (Chapter 6 will show you how), or by putting your message under a rock in the backyard or in the cracks of a tree down the street. But if you just hide a message, and it's in plain English, there's always a chance that the wrong person could find it. Yipes! Then anyone could be in on your secret plans.

The second, more secure way to keep a message secret is to make it hard to figure out—by using a secret code or cipher that only you and your friends know. Anyone else looking at it will see only mumbo-jumbo.

Codes and ciphers (which are codes made by scrambling letters) are ways of hiding the meaning of your message. Say you're planning a confidential meeting with your best friend. If you put a note saying "MEET ME AT THE PLAYGROUND" in your special hiding place, and the wrong person finds it, your meeting isn't very secret anymore. But if the message says "JBBQ JB XQ QEB MIXVDOLRKA," chances are your secret will be safe. This message is written in a very easy code, called a substitution cipher, that you'll find out about in Chapter 2. Ciphers like these are easy for you and your friends to understand, but much, much harder for anyone else to read.

You can use many different languages and codes to send your most secret messages: sign languages, Morse code, Braille, and picture languages like the ones on the tombs of the ancient Egyptians. You can even make up your own languages. You'll find lots of "code books" and "code machines" around your house waiting to be used. You can even use codes to perform magic tricks to amaze your family and friends. The secrets are all in this book.

But beware: people are always on the lookout for ways to break your codes and unlock the mysteries you create. So don't let this book fall into the wrong hands!

1 Codes Everywhere

The year is 1917. Europe is torn by war. German submarines prowl the waters around the British Isles, sinking English merchant ships. The Germans hope to starve the British into defeat, but supplies are still getting through on neutral American ships. The Germans want to sink these ships, too, but they don't want the United States getting involved in the war in Europe.

The Germans think up a sly plan. They ask Mexico to attack the United States in order to keep the United States busy defending itself. A German statesman, Arthur Zimmermann, sends a telegram, written in secret code, offering a big chunk of the United States to Mexico if Mexico will attack the United States.

The plan backfires. The British intercept the message and manage to decode it. They inform President Woodrow Wilson of Germany's offer to Mexico.

The American public is outraged, and the United States enters World War I against Germany.

No Smoking

No Asparagus

You may think of codes as secret, cloak-and-dagger mysteries. But a code is really any way that people agree to communicate. If you're thinking that this makes English a code, you're right!

The important thing about a code is that it has a key, a list of words or symbols that stand for something else. You hold the key to English because you know that each word stands for a certain object or action or idea. You know, for example, that the letters C-A-T stand for a small, furry animal that says "meow." You know that if someone shouts DUCK, there may be something whizzing toward your head and you'd better scrunch down quickly.

All languages are codes. They are *secret* codes when only a few people have the key. The Navaho Indians have their own language, and they don't think of it as a secret code because they all understand it. But in World War II, the United States Marines had Navaho radio operators send top secret messages to each other in Navaho because it wasn't very likely that the Germans would recognize or understand the language.

We use all kinds of codes every day without even thinking about them. Street signs and street lights are codes that everyone should know. A circle with a line through it is a common code for "no" or "forbidden."

YOUR OWN SECRET CODE WORDS AND CODE BOOKS

Maybe you've seen television shows about hospitals that use codes over the intercom: "Code blue, room 335." This code isn't secret; it's just a way of letting doctors and nurses know in a hurry that there's an emergency. Code blue or code 99 means that a patient has stopped breathing or her heart has stopped beating, so help is needed—and quickly.

You can invent your own code using names of colors. If you tell your friends what certain colors stand for, you can give secret messages to each other that nobody else will understand. On the telephone, for example, "code red" could mean "I can't talk about this now, somebody's listening. Let's change the subject." Code green could mean "All clear." Code blue could mean "Quick! Hide the invisible ink! My little brother is coming!"

When you write something in code, you are *encoding*. When you translate it back into English, that's called *decoding*. As you make up more and more code words, you'll want to keep a list of them and what they stand for. This is your key, or your code book. Give a copy of the key to your friends so they can decode your messages. You can even use misleading or silly words to stand for things, so your messages are harder for an outsider to figure out. Part of your key might look like this:

BIRDS	= RECORDS
CAMEL	= BICYCLE
HOUSE	= PLAYGROUND

```
KICK      = GO TO
STOP      = PLAY
POPCORN = BASKETBALL
TREE      = HOUSE
```

Maybe you'd like to play basketball and then listen to records this afternoon. Using the secret code above, you could send a message that only your friends could figure out. It might look like this:

LET'S KICK THE HOUSE ON OUR
CAMELS AND STOP POPCORN,
THEN WE CAN KICK MY TREE
AND LISTEN TO BIRDS.

If you're worried that somebody might find your code book, use a different code book that no one will suspect—a dictionary. Here's how it works:

If your message is MEET ME AT THE PARK, look up the word MEET in your dictionary. On a sheet of paper, write the number of the page where you found MEET. Then count down the number of words defined on that page until you reach MEET, and write that number, too. Put a dash between these two numbers.

If MEET is the fourth word defined on page 441, and ME is the 17th word on page 438, the beginning of your message will look like this:

441–4 438–17

Tell your friend the secret of the code, and your friend can look up each word in the dictionary. But make sure your friend has exactly the same edition of the dictionary or you won't be able to decode each other's messages!

COMPUTER CODES

These days, it's important that computers be able to "talk" to one another. Most people think of computers as being very smart machines, but in some ways computers are not so smart, because they can recognize only two things—ON and OFF. This is because computers use electricity to compute, and electricity is either on or off, like a lamp. So computers need a code that can translate everything into On/Off terms. This code is *binary code,* and it describes everything in ones and zeros. In binary code, the numbers zero through nine look like this:

0 = 0000	5 = 0101
1 = 0001	6 = 0110
2 = 0010	7 = 0111
3 = 0011	8 = 1000
4 = 0100	9 = 1001

The letters of the alphabet also have to be coded with ones and zeros for a computer to read. So that computers can exchange information, a binary code has been developed that is shared by practically all of the computers in the United States. It's called ASCII (pronounced ASK-EE), which stands for American Standard Code for Information Interchange. ASCII uses a set of seven ones and zeros for each letter and symbol found on a typical computer keyboard. For example, a capital *A* is always 1000001 and a small *a* is always 1100001 in ASCII. That way, all the computers with the key to ASCII can exchange information, just the way you and I can understand each other because we hold the key to English.

2

Ciphers

In "The Adventure of the Dancing Men" by Arthur Conan Doyle, the puzzling stick figures on page 19 are sent to Sherlock Holmes. The famous detective enlists the help of his good friend, Dr. Watson, to help him figure them out:

"Every problem becomes very childish when once it is explained to you. Here is an unexplained one. See what you can make of that, friend Watson."
He tossed a sheet of paper upon the table, and turned once more to his chemical analysis.

I looked in amazement at the absurd hieroglyphics upon the paper.
"Why, Holmes, it is a child's drawing," I cried.
"Oh, that's your idea!"
"What else could it be?"

What else indeed? Of course, Sherlock Holmes is able to figure out what the little figures are. They are a secret message written in cipher, which means that each dancing stick figure stands for a letter of the alphabet.

Codes are not always secret, but ciphers almost always are. A cipher is a way to rearrange or change the letters of a message according to a key that only the sender and the

receiver know. The key is usually easy to memorize so that you can encode and decode the message without a code list or code book. That way, there's nothing to fall into enemy hands.

There are two ways to transform your message using a cipher. You can scramble the letters of the message so that they are out of order. This is called a *transposition cipher.* For example, if you unscramble the letters in PLEAP, you can get the word APPLE.

The second way to create a cipher is to substitute different letters, numbers, or signs for each letter in your message. This is called a *substitution cipher.*

You could rearrange the letters DSSOH as much as you like, but you'll never get them to spell APPLE

because each letter stands for a different letter. In this example, D stands for A, S stands for P, O stands for L, and H stands for E. The cipher that Sherlock Holmes figures out in "The Adventure of the Dancing Men" is another type of substitution cipher.

TRANSPOSITION CIPHERS
Can you read this message?

ELBUORT NI UOY ERA YOB

It's in the easiest cipher around! Try reading it backward:

BOY ARE YOU IN TROUBLE

You wouldn't want to use this backward cipher for your most secret messages, because it's much too easy to figure out. There are lots of better ways to rearrange letters into patterns to keep your message secure from prying eyes.

The Up-and-Down Cipher

Whenever you're going to write a message in cipher, you'll probably want to write it down in English first (on a different piece of paper than the one you're sending your message on, of course). Cryptologists call the unchanged message *plaintext*. The first step in putting the message into cipher, or enciphering, is to take out all the punctuation and spaces between the words of your message. Those spaces give too many clues.

By taking out spaces between words,

LOOK IN OUR SECRET HIDING PLACE
becomes
LOOKINOURSECRETHIDINGPLACE.

Next, count the number of letters in your message. You'll be dividing that number in half. If there is an odd number of letters, add any letter to the end—maybe an X. This extra letter has no meaning and is called a *null*.

Write the letters of the message on two lines, with the first letter on the upper line, the second letter on the lower line, and so on:

L O I O R E R T I I G L C
  O K N U S C E H D N P A E

Now write out the top line followed by the second line:

LOIORERTIIGLCOKNUSCEHDNPAE

Divide the letters into groups of any size you like:

LOI OR ERTI IGL COKNUS CEHD N PAE

Now your message looks very mysterious, maybe even like a foreign language. But you can tell a friend how to decode, or decipher, your message in a couple of minutes: just count the number of letters in the message (ignoring the spaces) and divide by two. For example, the message above has 26 letters. Tell your friend to write the first half of the message (in this example, the first 13 letters) on one line with spaces between the letters. Write the second half beneath those spaces:

L O I O R E R T I I G L C
  O K N U S C E H D N P A E

Then your friend can rewrite the message by slipping the lower letters into the spaces in the top line:

LOOKINOURSECRETHIDINGPLACE

All your friend has to do now is figure out where to put spaces between the words.

The Winding Way Cipher

The most common transposition ciphers use columns or grids to scramble the letters of the message. Once again, you'll want to write out the message without spaces between words.

OURNEWPASSWORDISELEPHANT

Next, count the letters in the message. This message has 24 letters. Now think of a pattern of columns and rows that these letters will fit. For example, 24 letters will fit into a grid of 24 squares (6 squares wide by 4 squares high) because $6 \times 4 = 24$. These letters will also fit into a 5 by 5 grid with one box to spare. Let's use 5 columns and 5 rows, and fill the boxes with the letters of the message from left to right, like this:

O	U	R	N	E
W	P	A	S	S
W	O	R	D	I
S	E	L	E	P
H	A	N	T	

There is an empty space in the last box. Put an X, your initial, or any null letter you like into that box. Using this grid (sometimes called a matrix), you can discover all kinds of winding ways to rearrange the letters of your message:

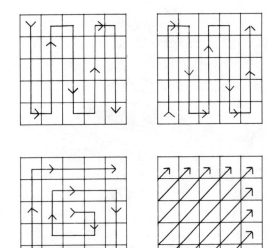

Encipher your message using the path you like best. Using the first pattern, for example, the message becomes:

OWWSHAEOPURARLNTEDSNESIPC

or

OWW SHAE OPUR ARLNTED SNE SIPC

How many other winding ways can you think of for this grid? You can send secret messages using each of them, but make sure your friends know which grid pattern you're using and how big the grid is so that they can fill up the boxes in the right order. Then they can read across the squares in order to decipher your message.

Suppose you found the following message in your secret hiding place:

TGYY ESMNA HET ESBB HW EDOMG OB

If you know that your key is a 5 by 5 grid, with a down-and-up winding path starting at the upper left, you'd fill in the letters like this:

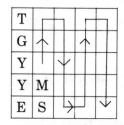

PARTIALLY FILLED-IN GRID

T	H	E	D	O
G	A	T	E	M
Y	N	E	W	G
Y	M	S	H	O
E	S	B	B	B

COMPLETED GRID

Reading across, the completed grid reveals the message:

THE DOG ATE MY NEW GYM SHOES BBB

(The three B's at the end are nulls.)

Key Word Columns

Here's another way to use columns to send messages. Pick a key word with five or six letters. (Make sure it's a word with no repeated letters. A word like PURPLE, with two P's, won't work.) Make a column for each letter in the key word. Say your key word for the day is SNACK and the message you want to send is HELP! I LOST MY CODE BOOK. Write SNACK across the top of a page and then write the message in columns under it like this:

```
S  N  A  C  K
H  E  L  P  I
L  O  S  T  M
Y  C  O  D  E
B  O  O  K  X
```

Then rearrange the columns so that the letters in your key word (SNACK) are in alphabetical order (ACKNS)

```
A  C  K  N  S
L  P  I  E  H
S  T  M  O  L
O  D  E  C  Y
O  K  X  O  B
```

Write the message by copying the letters down each column, not including the key word:

LSOO PTDK IMEX EOCO HLYB

To decipher the message, all your friends have to do is write the letters of the key word, SNACK, in alphabetical order and put the letters of your message in columns under it. Then they rearrange the columns so that the key word appears in its normal way. The message is then easy to read.

SUBSTITUTION CIPHERS

You can encipher and decipher any transposition cipher if you know how the letters of the message were scrambled. In a substitution cipher, a different kind of key is used. Here, each letter of the alphabet has a secret equivalent that replaces it in the coded message.

Number Ciphers

You can substitute numbers for letters to create a cipher. The most obvious way is to let A=1, B=2, C=3, and so on up to Z=26. But, as you can imagine, this is not a hard cipher to figure out.

A more clever way of using numbers is to make a 5 by 5 grid and put the letters of the alphabet into these boxes. Number the columns and rows like this:

COLUMN NUMBERS:

		1	2	3	4	5
ROW NUMBERS:	1	A	B	C	D	E
	2	F	G	H	I	J
	3	K	L	M	N	O
	4	P	Q	R	S	T
	5	U	V	W	X	Y Z

Since there are 26 letters in the alphabet and only 25 squares, we have to fit both Y and Z into the last box. (This shouldn't cause too much confusion since the letter Z isn't used very often.)

To write your message in this number code, use the row numbers and the column numbers as directions to where to find each letter. If your message starts with the letter N, look for N in the grid. It's in row 3, under column 4, so the code number for N is 34.

Read this message using the grid:

24 31 34 35 53 53 23 35 45 23 43 15 53
45 23 11 45 14 24 43 45 12 35 33 12

This secret code is sometimes called the *Polybius cipher* after the ancient Greek who first thought of using 25 squares of a grid to stand for the letters of the alphabet. (The message says I KNOW WHO THREW THAT DIRT BOMB.)

Shift Ciphers

You can also make up a cipher by "shifting" the letters of one alphabet against another alphabet, as in figure A.

Then take the first three letters of the column 1 (ABC) and put them beside the last three letters of column 2 (XYZ) as in figure B.

Column 1 of figure B is your cipher alphabet. Column 2 is your plaintext alphabet. To encode your message, find the letters of your message in column 2 but write down the cipher letter next to it in column 1. So, this message:

ARE YOU READY FOR THE TEST TOMORROW

becomes:

DUH BRX UHDGB IRU WKH WHVW WRPRUURZ

These ciphers, usually called shift ciphers, are also known as *Julius Caesar ciphers*, because the Roman Emperor Caesar is said to have used such codes. The shift can be any number of letters, but be sure that the receiver knows how many letters to shift.

FIGURE A

Column 1	Column 2
A	
B	
C	
D	A
E	B
F	C
G	D
H	E
I	F
J	G
K	H
L	I
M	J
N	K
O	L
P	M
Q	N
R	O
S	P
T	Q
U	R
V	S
W	T
X	U
Y	V
Z	W
	X
	Y
	Z

FIGURE B

Column 1	Column 2
D	A
E	B
F	C
G	D
H	E
I	F
J	G
K	H
L	I
M	J
N	K
O	L
P	M
Q	N
R	O
S	P
T	Q
U	R
V	S
W	T
X	U
Y	V
Z	W
A	X
B	Y
C	Z

FIGURE C

C
R
A
Z
Y
B
D
E
F
G
H
I
J
K
L
M
N
O
P
Q
S
T
U
V
W
X

FIGURE D

C	A
R	B
A	C
Z	D
Y	E
B	F
D	G
E	H
F	I
G	J
H	K
I	L
J	M
K	N
L	O
M	P
N	Q
O	R
P	S
Q	T
S	U
T	V
U	W
V	X
W	Y
X	Z

Shift ciphers are well known, but there are ways of putting an extra "spin" in your shift to make it difficult for anyone to figure out. One way is to include a secret password in your cipher. Your secret password might be CRAZY. (Make sure it's a word with no repeated letters. Also, pick a word that has a letter that appears late in the alphabet, such as U, V, W, X, Y, or Z.) Write your secret password, and then all the letters of the alphabet minus the ones in that word, as in figure C.

Then write the entire plaintext alphabet next to it, as in figure D.

Tell your friends how to make up this key using your secret password. Then you can write messages by replacing each letter in your plaintext message with the letter next to it in the cipher alphabet:

JSPQ BFKZ KYU EFZYLSQ
—PLJYLKY BLIILUYZ SP QL QEY LIZ LKY

(This message says, MUST FIND NEW HIDEOUT—SOMEONE FOLLOWED US TO THE OLD ONE.)

The Pigpen Cipher

⌐⌐⌐⌐ ⌐⌐ ⌐ ⌐⌐⌐ ⌐⌐⌐

This secret message looks pretty strange, doesn't it? You might think it was a foreign alphabet or some ancient magic symbols. But it's an ingenious cipher that translates very easily into English once you know the secret. It was developed hundreds of years ago, and variations of it have been used by a secret society called the Freemasons and by Confederate soldiers during the American Civil War.

Here's how to use the easiest version of it. Draw two tick-tack-toe boards and two big X's. Put dots inside the second tick-tack-toe board and the second X, like this:

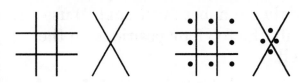

Fill all the compartments with the letters of the alphabet, like this:

A	B	C		J		N•	O•	P•		W
D	E	F	M	K		Q•	R•	S•	Z	X
G	H	I		L		T•	U•	V•		Y

Now you're ready to use the pigpen cipher. Use the shape of the compartment around each letter to draw the cipher letters (A is ⌐ and B is ⌶).

The word MYSTERY looks like this:

>∧⊡ ·⊓☐⊡∧

You can change the letters inside the compartments any way you like, just so long as you remember where you put them. To decipher a pigpen message, compare the cipher letters to the various compartments. (Be sure you and your friends are using the same patterns.)

By now, you've probably figured out the message written in pigpen cipher at the beginning of this section. It says PIGPEN IS A SILLY NAME.

USING BRAILLE AS A CIPHER

Braille is a touch alphabet that was developed to help the blind read. This alphabet uses raised dots that can be "read" with the fingers. It was developed by Louis Braille in 1824, when he was 15 years old.

Blinded in an accident when he was three, Braille went to school with children who could see, and learned by memorizing everything his teachers told him. The only books available for blind people at the time were huge bulky things in which the letters of the alphabet were raised and enlarged so that the students could feel them. Braille heard about a system of raised dots and dashes that the French army was developing for soldiers who needed to read important messages at night. The army's system was too complicated, so Braille created a simple one. He came up with a system based on a pattern of six dots, called a cell, that looks like this:

Here's how the Braille alphabet is put together. The first ten letters of the alphabet (A through J) use only the top four positions on the cell:

A   B   C   D   E

F   G   H   I   J

The second ten letters of the alphabet (K–T) add the bottom left dot of the cell to those same patterns:

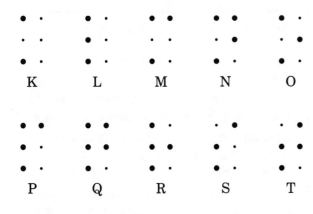

K   L   M   N   O

P   Q   R   S   T

The letters U, V, X, Y and Z use both bottom dots:

U   V   X   Y   Z

And W looks like this:

W

You can use braille as a written cipher simply by drawing these dot combinations on a piece of paper.

RANDOM SUBSTITUTION CIPHERS

In a random substitution cipher, you can substitute anything you like, in any order, for each letter of the alphabet. This makes it hard for a nosy outsider to break your cipher, but also harder for you to remember it. Once you make up your random substitution cipher, you'll need to keep a copy of it with you to encipher and decipher messages.

To make up a random cipher, write all the letters of the alphabet and put any letter, number, or symbol you like beside each one. You might want to use the symbols on a typewriter, like this:

A	!	F	˜	K	:	Q	%	V	.
B	@	G	)	L	{	R	–	W	/
C	*	H	?	M	;	S	&	X	<
D	+	I	,	N	"	T	=	Y	'
E	×	J	½	O	(	U	>	Z	}
				P	#				

Or you might want to make up your own set of symbols, which might look something like this:

A	○	F	⊥	K	⊙	Q	▣	V	☆
B	□	G	ℳ	L	⊠	R	⌇	W	←
C	●	H	↑	M	↓	S	∞	X	◑
D	⚹	I	+	N	▽	T	→	Y	▱
E	◉	J	◇	O	△	U	◬	Z	◒
				P	ℳ				

HOW TO CRACK A CIPHER

Suppose you've just intercepted a message in a secret code. It looks, from the way the letters are grouped, like it's a simple substitution cipher—maybe a shift cipher or a random substitution cipher. How would you crack it?

You could start by trying different shift ciphers at random, but this could take a long time. If the code isn't a shift cipher after all, you could go through all 25 shifted alphabets and get nowhere. Clearly, you need to look for some other kinds of clues.

Fortunately, people who specialize in cracking ciphers have discovered some facts about the English language that can help you crack someone else's cipher. The most important thing to know is how often particular letters and words are likely to show up in a message. The most commonly used letter in the

English language is E, and the second most common is T. So if one letter shows up in your message much more often than any other, it's likely to be an E, or perhaps a T.

Here's the entire alphabet, arranged from the most frequently used letters to the least frequently used:

E T A O N R I S H D L F M C U G Y P W B V K X J Q Z

The most commonly used words in the English language are:

THE, OF, AND, TO, IN, A, IS, THAT, FOR, IT.

Here are some other hints about English that can provide clues to cracking someone's code:

- If there's a single-letter word in the message, it's probably either A or I (occasionally, it might be O)
- T is the most common first letter of a word
- E is the most common last letter of a word
- Q is always followed by U
- The most common double letters are LL, EE, OO, TT, and FF

If you'd like to see Sherlock Holmes put these principles to work, read "The Adventure of the Dancing Men," by Arthur Conan Doyle. And if you'd like to practice cracking ciphers yourself, look in the newspaper for "Cryptograms," which are sometimes found in the comics section. These are sayings that have been put into ciphers.

3 Code Machines

In the years before the United States entered World War II, American intelligence agents listened closely to Japanese radio signals. Because the Japanese codes weren't too complicated, the messages weren't difficult to decode. Then, in 1939, the Japanese started using a new and baffling cipher for their top secret messages. The Americans set about cracking this frustrating new code, which they called Purple.

It took more than a year of hard work before the Americans figured out how Purple worked. It was a cipher created by two interconnected typewriters. As the plaintext message was typed into one typewriter, electrical signals were sent through a maze of complicated wiring to rotating disks in the other typewriter. These disks continually changed the cipher alphabet as they typed out the secret message. Because the alphabet changed constantly, the Japanese were confident that their machine cipher was unbreakable.

But the Americans had to try. Working backward from the coded messages, the Americans painstakingly pieced together a working replica of the Purple machine—without ever having seen one. They did such a good job that their Purple machine actually worked faster than the Japanese machine!

Unfortunately, breaking the Purple code was not enough to prevent the

PURPLE MACHINE

disastrous attack on Pearl Harbor in 1941. Two years later, however, Purple provided the Americans with an opportunity for revenge. An intercepted message revealed that the man who had led the attack on Pearl Harbor was on his way to a secret meeting in the Pacific. Armed with this knowledge, the Americans were able to shoot down his plane.

The Purple machine, with all of its rotating disks and changeable wiring, was very complicated. Imagine how much more complicated modern computerized code machines have become. Of course, we can't know exactly how complicated they are, because they're still top secret!

You don't need a computer to have a code machine. You can find lots of things at home that will make great secret coders and decoders—like your telephone, for example.

TELEPHONE CODE MACHINE

Take a look at your telephone. It probably looks like the one shown on the next page.

The numbers 2 through 9 are each positioned below three letters. You can use those numbers and letters to write secret messages to your friends. Notice that the dial or buttons don't have any letters for the numbers 1 or 0. This is fine, because there also aren't any numbers for Q or Z. So you can use 1 for Q and 0 for Z.

Say you want to encode the word

GO. On the telephone, G is the first letter over number 4. So you use a 4 with a dot to the left of it for G, like this: ·4. The third letter over number 6 is O, so it is encoded as 6·. So you see, GO=·4 6·. If the letter you want to use is a middle letter, such as B or N, put the dot over the number: B=2̇, and N=6̇.

What does this say?

·7 4̇ 6· 6̇ 3̇   4̇ 6· ·6 3̇

MAKE A SCYTALE

The ancient Greeks invented a very simple machine for coding and decoding secret messages that needed to be brought into the scene of a battle. It was called a scytale (see-TAHL-ee), and nobody seeing one for the first time would suspect that it was a code machine.

The scytale was simply a cylinder of wood—perhaps the battle commander's staff. The Greeks would wrap a long piece of paper around the cylinder in a spiral, and then write a message across each turn of the paper, as on page 38. When the paper was unwrapped, nobody could read it without first wrapping it around a cylinder of the same thickness as the original.

If you can find two cylinders of the same size, you and your friends can send messages the way the Greeks did. Juice cans and the cardboard rolls from toilet paper or paper towels work well. Maybe you can persuade your mom or dad to saw an old broom handle into a couple of pieces to make sturdier scytales for you.

You'll need extra-long paper cut into thin strips to write your messages. Try cutting out the margins of a newspaper, or buy some adding-machine paper at the stationery store. Simply wind your strip of paper around your scytale, write your message across it, unwrap the message, and send it off to someone with the same size scytale.

THE CIPHER WHEEL

A cipher wheel is another code machine you can make. You'll need:
- tracing paper • cardboard
- paste • a tack
- scissors • an eraser

Trace the two circles on page 39 onto the tracing paper.

Paste the circles onto the cardboard and cut them out when they dry. Put the smaller one on top of the larger one, so that it fits inside.

Push the tack through the

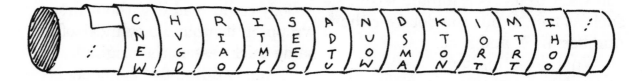

center of both wheels, and then stick the point of the tack into the eraser.

And there you have it—a machine that will let you use any shift cipher you like without writing everything down.

The outside disk is your cipher alphabet. The inside disk is your plaintext alphabet. To make your cipher, decide what you want your key letter to be. Find that letter on the outside disk, and whirl the inside disk around until the A matches up with your key letter. To encode a message, find each letter of your message on the inside disk, but write down the letter on the outside disk.

Have your friends make their own cipher disks that are identical to yours. Think of ways to let them

know which key letter you're using for each message—maybe by writing that letter in the pigpen cipher at the beginning of your message. Then your friends can decode your message by using the cipher alphabet on the outside disk to discover the plaintext letters on the inside disk.

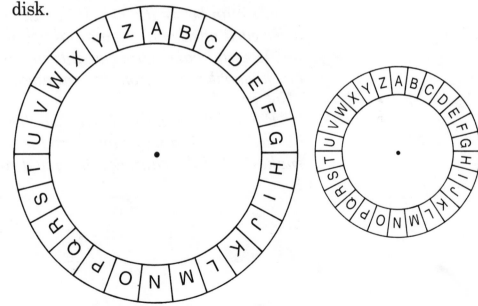

4 Signals and Sign Languages

In St. Peter's Square in Rome, a hushed crowd gathers outside the Vatican, the home of the Pope. All eyes are on a Vatican chimney, watching for a puff of smoke. Will it be white or black?

Inside the Vatican, the cardinals are gathered. The Pope has died, and the church officials must select a new Pope. Two-thirds of them must agree on one man before the new Pope can be declared. The ballots are tallied twice each afternoon. Again and again, the officials are unable to agree. The unsuccessful ballots are cast into the fire and burned, causing a plume of black smoke to rise from the chimney, telling the people gathered outside, "Not yet. . ."

Finally, the majority is reached. The last and deciding set of ballots is burned in such a way that it produces white smoke. When the white smoke snakes out of the chimney, the crowd roars, knowing that they have a new Pope.

All of the codes and ciphers we've used so far are for written or spoken messages. But sometimes it isn't possible to get a written or spoken message to someone. Maybe you want to reach a lot of people at once with important news, like the news of a new Pope. Or maybe you want to send messages under special circumstances: when you can't talk or write; when you're too far away from the person you need to get a message to; or when it's too dark to read or write. That's when signals and sign languages come in handy.

Battlegrounds have historically been the places where signals have been put to use. Imagine that you're the commander of a legion of soldiers at war. Noise and confusion are everywhere. You need to get everyone to charge at the enemy, but you know you won't be heard above the hubbub, even if you shout. You obviously can't send a written or spoken message from soldier to soldier. What do you do?

Alexander the Great used an array of signals to order his troops about—trumpets, flags, swords, torches, and even smoke signals. Julius Caesar used musical instruments to give orders in battle: horns and tubas directed the foot soldiers, while higher-pitched trumpets commanded the cavalry. During the American Civil War, a system of waving flags, called wigwag, was used by both Union and Confederate troops.

FLAG CODES

Before the invention of radio, communication between ships at sea presented a problem because ships don't usually pass close enough to one another to make letter-passing or shouting practical. So various navies came up with different systems of flag signals to communicate ship-to-ship. Today, the International Code of Signals, made up of colorful flags that stand for individual numbers and letters, is used by ships to get messages to one another.

Flags can come in handy for you, too. Using brightly colored construction paper, you and your friends can make up a system of flags for sending important messages. You can tape these flags to the window in your room to leave messages for your friends when you aren't home. A green flag could mean "Gone to the playground." A blue flag could

mean "Gone to the library." Then your friends would know where to find you. You could also use flags if you couldn't get out of the house for some reason. A red flag could mean "I can't come out—I've got to do homework." For really desperate times, you could have a black flag with a white cross or a skull and crossbones on it, meaning "Don't bother knocking—Mom says I'm grounded for life."

SEMAPHORE

Another system of flag signals used on ships is semaphore. Instead of using a different flag to stand for each letter, the semaphore alphabet uses two identical flags held at different angles to represent letters and numbers. This is how the semaphore alphabet looks:

44

Semaphore Alphabet

Attention

 A

 B

 C

 D

 E

F

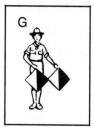 G

H

 I

 J

 K

 L

 M

 N

 O

 P

 Q

 R

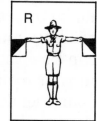

You can make your own semaphore flags by cutting a large piece of white posterboard into squares. Make sure your squares are big enough to be seen at a distance—at least 1 foot square. With a ruler, draw a diagonal line from corner to corner on each square, like this:

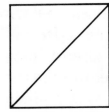

Paint one half of each square black, like this:

Once the flags are dry, you can start practicing your semaphore alphabet.

SIGNALING WITH MORSE CODE

Samuel Morse had a problem. He had just invented the telegraph, a machine that could send electrical impulses over wires across great distances. He could press a button and, almost instantly, a click would be heard miles away. This, he felt sure, was a much cheaper and faster way of sending messages than by mail or pony express. But his machine would only send clicks, not words. Morse needed a click language before his invention would be useful to anyone. So he set about devising one of his own.

Morse decided that his language would be based on two kinds of clicks: short clicks (dots) and long clicks (dashes). By visiting his neighborhood printing shop, Morse learned which letters of the alphabet are used most frequently in the English language. These he assigned the simplest click combinations. E, for example, is just a dot. Here is the entire Morse alphabet:

A	• —	J	• — — —	R	• — •
B	— • • •	K	— • —	S	• • •
C	— • — •	L	• — • •	T	—
D	— • •	M	— —	U	• • —
E	•	N	— •	V	• • • —
F	• • — •	O	— — —	W	• — —
G	— — •	P	• — — •	X	— • • —
H	• • • •	Q	— — • —	Y	— • — —
I	• •			Z	— — • •

The neat thing about Morse code is that you don't need a telegraph to use it. You can use almost anything that makes a sound. Try practicing Morse code by rapping on a table. Try plunking it on a piano, tooting it on a flute, or tapping it on a drum. If you and your brother or sister have been sent to your rooms, and your rooms are next to each other, you can send messages by tapping on the wall. Not too loud, though—you don't want everyone in the house to know you're sending messages!

Not only sounds but light can be used to send Morse code. At night, you and a friend can take flash-lights outside to send messages. Flick the flashlight on and off, or just cover and uncover the lens with your hand or a piece of cardboard to let out short flashes for dots and longer flashes for dashes.

INDIAN SIGN LANGUAGE

Long before European settlers came to this continent, tribes of Indians flourished throughout the North American plains. Each of the dozens of tribes had its own language and customs, but members of different tribes would often band together to trade or hunt buffalo. There was rarely enough time while hot on the trail of game to learn one anothers' language, but the Indians had little trouble understanding each other. An ancient language of signs and gestures, developed through centuries of trading and hunting, warring, and making peace, was shared by all of the tribes.

The sign language of the Plains Indians

Trade

Joke

Noon

Know

Sleep

Water

Some of the signs the Plains Indians used are shown above.

It's easy to see where the Indians got the idea for many of their signs. Like the Indians, you can make up your own sign language. Imagine you're trying to communicate with someone who doesn't speak any English—what kinds of signs would you come up

Many

Hungry

Tepee

Horse

Bird

Friend

with to be sure you're understood? How would you ask what time it was? Could you use signs to show what your favorite sports are? What signs would you use for words like HOUSE, RUN, FAMILY, DOG, EAT, and FLY? How would you use signs to show emotions like happy, sad, angry, surprised?

American Sign Language manual alphabet

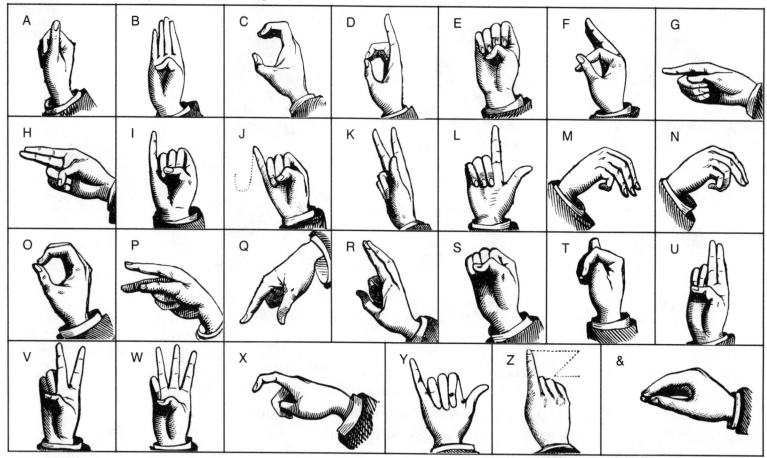

AMERICAN SIGN LANGUAGE

A different kind of sign language is "spoken" by about half a million people in the U.S. and Canada for a special reason—they cannot hear. The gesture language of the deaf in this country is called American Sign Language (sometimes called ASL or Ameslan).

Like the sign language of the Plains Indians, American Sign Language has signs that stand for complete words and thoughts. But ASL also has an alphabet you can learn to use, called a *manual alphabet*.

Try signing your name using the ASL alphabet. This is called *fingerspelling*. Keep practicing until you can do it quickly.

If you'd like to learn about the signs that stand for words and ideas in ASL, you can find books on the subject in your library. Using these signs is much faster and easier than fingerspelling everything.

In the meantime, just in case you should meet a deaf person you'd like to say "Hi" to, here's how:

HI   MY   NAME

Then fingerspell your name. You don't need to say "is"—it's understood.

5 Picture Languages

It is 1799. The French Army, under Napoleon Bonaparte, has invaded Egypt. Some of the army is encamped near the small Egyptian town of Rosetta. One day, an engineering officer wandering near the encampment notices a slab of black stone partially buried in the mud. Curious, he brushes off some of the mud and takes a closer look.

To his amazement, the stone is covered with carvings. Some of them look like pictures, some like strange languages. Little does the officer know what he has stumbled upon—the key to the long-lost picture language of the ancient Egyptians.

Tens of thousands of years ago, long before humans invented written language, they felt the need to express themselves and record important events. They did this by drawing and painting pictures on rocks and on the walls of caves.

A hunter might celebrate his triumphant hunt by drawing scenes of his battle with the animal.

Eventually, people realized that simpler versions of these drawings could be used to stand for words or thoughts. Instead of drawing the

whole scene, the hunter could use a simple picture to convey his triumph:

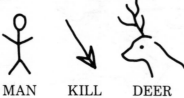

MAN   KILL   DEER

But a complete language made up of a different picture for each word probably never developed. Can you think why? Imagine how long it would take you to think up a different picture for each word in the English language. There are just too many of them! But even languages with thousands and thousands of words use only a few sounds. At some point along the road to written language, people realized that the pictures could stand for sounds instead of words—and so there could be fewer pictures to memorize.

A system of language that uses pictures to represent sounds is called *rebus writing*. In English, an example of rebus writing might look like this:

Can you figure out what it means? Try sounding it out: EYE CAN KNOT FLY (I cannot fly).

Once people realized that pictures could stand for sounds, the development of alphabets wasn't far off.

HIEROGLYPHICS
The ancient Egyptians carved a kind of picture writing into their

great monuments that used both rebuses that represented sounds, and pictures that stood for words and ideas. This mysterious and beautiful language is called *hieroglyphics* (HI-ro-GLIF-iks), which means "sacred carving" in Greek.

The fancy hieroglyphics of the ancient Egyptians gave way to simpler alphabets, and the meanings of the sacred carvings were lost for centuries. Nobody even knew for sure whether the hieroglyphics were a real language or just decorations. Not until the French army officer made his lucky discovery of the Rosetta stone in 1799 was anyone able to make head or tail of the pictures on the ancient monuments.

The Rosetta stone, which dated back almost to 200 B.C., had a

The Rosetta Stone was the key to deciphering ancient Egyptian hieroglyphics.

message carved in it in three different languages: Greek, hieroglyphics, and another, simpler Egyptian language. Since Greek was a known language, this stone held the key to the mysterious hieroglyphics.

Many people tried their hand at deciphering the stone, with little success. Not until Jean Francois Champollion, a French historian who specialized in languages, studied the stone did it yield up its secrets. Champollion was a real whiz at languages: he knew six ancient languages by the time he was 12 years old.

Certain groups of pictures on the stone had rings around them. People who had tried to read the puzzling stone had supposed that these were the names of Egyptian rulers, but they had only been able to figure out one of them. Fortunately for Champollion, someone discovered another stone that had similar ringed pictures and a helpful translation in Greek. The Greek part mentioned the famous Cleopatra, so Champollion looked for a ringed set of symbols that might be Cleopatra's name. He found the symbols you see on page 56.

Hoping that this picture was Cleopatra's name in hieroglyphics, Champollion numbered the pictures and assigned the sounds of Cleopatra's name to each, like this:

| C | RW = L | I |

Using these clues, Champollion went back to the Rosetta stone and worked out the sounds of the other pictures. He went on to decipher many of the inscriptions on the tombs of the pharaohs using the clues he discovered in the Rosetta stone.

You can create your own picture language and make hieroglyphics one of your secret codes. Draw a simple picture for each letter of the alphabet. You might want to use pictures of things that begin with the letters they stand for, like having an apple stand for A and a baseball stand for B, like this:

A   B   C

Then the word "cab" would look like this:

PICTURE LANGUAGES OF HOBOS AND INDIANS

Another kind of picture language is one used by hobos and gypsies around the world. Wandering from town to town, hobos would leave signs in inconspicuous places to tell other wanderers what they could expect to find there—fierce dogs, a hot meal, a place to sleep. Here are some of the hobo signs and their meanings.

Because the hobo language is secret, the signs aren't very easy for someone unfamiliar with them to understand.

Hobo Signs

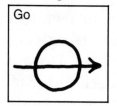
Go

Doctor

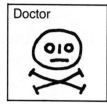
Bad dog

Very good

Guarded house

Stop

Indian Signs

Danger	Tell a pitiful story	Sun	Man	Tree
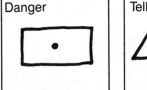	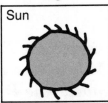	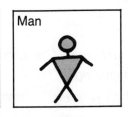	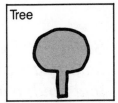	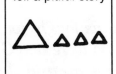

Be quiet	Woman	Two people talking	Listening	Crying
			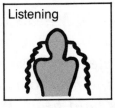	

A different kind of wanderer—the American Plains Indians—developed a picture language that was meant to be easy to read, not a secret. The Plains Indians used this picture language, along with the sign language you saw in Chapter 4, to communicate with Indians from other tribes who didn't speak their language. You can see how almost anyone could quickly learn to "speak" the Indian picture language.

You can use the picture languages of the hobos and the Indians to leave messages in chalk around the neighborhood for your friends. Get books out of the library to learn more of the pictures that these wanderers used. Or you may want to invent your own picture language. If you want your messages to be secret, your pictures shouldn't look too much like what they stand for, or anyone could read them.

6

Hiding the Message

Some 2,500 years ago, the Greeks and the Persians fought for control of the land that we now call Turkey. Miletus and Sestos were two Greek cities in that land, but they were surrounded—the Persians controlled the countryside around them.

The governor of Miletus desperately needed to send a secret message to his Greek friend in Sestos, but he was afraid that anyone carrying a message would be searched by Persian troops. Then he hit upon a clever plan.

He shaved the head of one of his slaves and tattooed his secret message onto the slave's bald head. When the slave's hair grew back and concealed the message, the governor sent him off to Miletus, safe in the knowledge that the Persians could search him and find no message.

When the slave reached the governor's friend in Sestos, he told him to shave his head again, and the message was revealed. Pleased with the success of this method, the Greeks continued to used head-shaving to send messages back and forth under the noses of the Persians.

Eventually, however, the Persians had enough of the Greeks and their secrets. In 494 B.C., they sacked the city of Miletus.

People have been finding ways of concealing their most important messages since prehistoric times. Some primitive people drew their sacred pictures in deep, dark caves, where only they and their kinsmen could find the pictures and understand their significance.

The process of hiding the message is called *steganography* (STEG-uh-NOG-ruh-fee) by cryptologists, and there's no limit to the number of ways you can think up to hide messages. Here are some ways to try your own hand at steganography. Don't worry, they're a lot more convenient than head shaving and cave painting.

INVISIBLE INKS

All kinds of citrus juices make good invisible inks. Pour some lemon juice, orange juice, or grapefruit juice into a small bowl. Use a cotton swab or a toothpick as a pen. Dip it into your ink and write your message on a blank piece of paper. If you're using a toothpick, don't bear down too hard or you might leave visible scratches on the paper. You'll have to write fairly quickly, because you'll only be able to see the words while they're wet!

You and your friends can make your invisible messages reappear by applying heat. The best way is with a 150-watt light bulb. Let the bulb warm up for a few minutes, then move the paper slowly over the top of the bulb and watch your message reappear. The letters will turn brown. Be careful not to touch the bulb with your fingers—it's hot!

If you don't have any citrus juice,

you can try vinegar. It works the same way, but doesn't develop as clearly as juice. Or you can try grating up a piece of onion and adding a little water to it. Onion juice works well, but it can make your eyes sting. And it sure stinks up the kitchen!

Sending a blank piece of paper with an invisible message on it may look suspicious and tip off the wrong people that you're using invisible ink. Here's how you can throw them off: Before you write your secret message in invisible ink, write a phony message on the paper using a pencil or pen. Be sure to leave space between the lines of your phony message—that's where you'll put the invisible message. If you want to be doubly secret, you can write the invisible message in one of your secret ciphers.

WATERMARKS

Watermarks use pressure instead of juice to make an invisible message. Dip a sheet of paper into water. Press the wet paper against your bathroom mirror or a window pane. Put a dry sheet over it, and write your message on the dry sheet in ballpoint pen. Press firmly. Throw out the top sheet with the visible message. See how your message has been pressed into the wet paper? Peel this sheet off the mirror and let it dry. When it dries, the message will disappear. To bring it back, wet the paper again.

You may want to scribble a phony message on the paper so it

doesn't look suspiciously blank, but be sure to use waterproof ink or pencil for the phony message so that it won't run and mess up your secret message when you wet the paper again.

RED FILTER MESSAGES

Here's another way to use a phony message to hide the presence of a secret one. You'll need a red pencil, a blue pencil, and a small sheet of transparent red cellophane—all of which you'll find at a stationery store. (Some report covers are made of clear red plastic that will work perfectly.)

Write your secret message on a piece of paper with the blue pencil. Don't press too hard—write faintly. Then use your red pencil to write your not-so-secret, phony message over the blue message, so that the secret message is difficult to read. Put the red cellophane over the message and see what happens: The red letters disappear, and the blue message stands out.

Be sure your friend has some red cellophane when you send the message, but don't send it along with the message or someone is bound to catch on to your secret.

SECRET GRIDS

You can hide one message inside another message if you use a secret grid with holes cut out of it. Big index cards—the 5″ by 7″ ones—are especially good for making secret grids. Draw word-sized rectangles on one of the index cards at different places, like figure 1 on page 65.

Cut out these rectangular holes. Now you need a second copy of this grid to give to a friend, so hold this card over another index card and trace the rectangular holes. Cut them out of the second card, too. Give this card to your friend.

To write a secret message, put the grid over a piece of paper. Fill up the holes with the words of your secret message. Put a dot at two of the corners of the index card to show your friend where his or her grid should go. Then take off the grid and fill in the spaces between the words of your message with other words. You can make it a very ordinary message, or a silly one, as in figure 2.

Only your friends with a secret grid identical to yours will know the real meaning of your message.

Figure 1

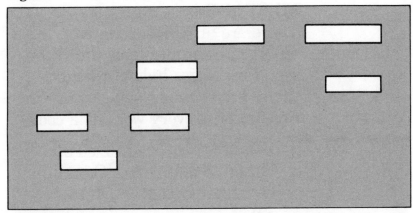

Figure 2

DEAR JOHN,
    DO YOU KNOW THE SECRET OF MEETING NEW FRIENDS? SOMETIMES YOU CAN FIND THEM AT THE PLAYGROUND. I FOUND MY VERY BEST FRIEND IN A TREE. HE WAS COLD, SO I TOOK HIM BACK TO MY HOUSE FOR THREE CUPS OF HOT CHOCOLATE. BUT HE HAD TO BE BACK IN HIS TREE AT 5 O'CLOCK, OTHERWISE HE WOULD TURN INTO A PUMPKIN.
                    CAROL

MESSAGES WITHIN MESSAGES

There are all kinds of ways of writing phony messages that have secret messages hidden within them. For example, you can use the first letter of every word as a code:

HONEST, I DIDN'T EVER TELL HENRY EVERYTHING. CAROL OVERHEARD DENNIS, ELLEN SAYS.

Run all the first letters of these words together and you have HIDETHECODES or HIDE THE CODES.

Try to think of other ways to hide messages within messages. You can use the first or last word in each sentence, or every fourth word, or the last letter in each word. The possibilities are endless!

Here's another way to bury one message inside another. Take a piece of paper and fold it into thirds. Write the words of your message down the folds, like this:

Fill up the rest of the page with a phony message, like this:

> BOB,
>
> MY NEW BIKE CAN BE FUN.
> IF I PASS, I'LL BE SURE TO SAY
> THE WORD. WANT TO RIDE IT?
> JOHN IS GOING TO TELL ON US,
> THAT CLOWN. TELL SALLY HI.
>
> KIM

Tell your friend where to look for the real message.

THE SECRET GRAPH

The secret graph will make your messages look like meaningless zig-zags to anyone not in on the secret.

To turn ordinary graph paper into a secret graph key, write the alphabet down one side of it, as shown. Make copies and give them to your friends.

To write a message using the secret graph, line up another piece of graph paper alongside the key. If your message is HELLO, put a dot where the first vertical line (that's an up-and-down line) crosses the H line, another dot where the second vertical line crosses the E line, and so on. Use a ruler to connect the dots. The message will look like the graph on the right.

NEWSPAPER DOTS AND PINPRICKS

About 150 years ago, people in England used newspapers to send messages to each other in the mail.

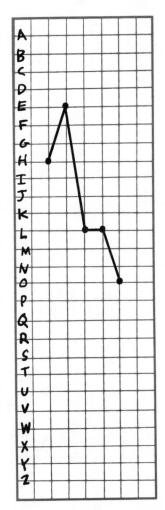

CAPE TOWN, SOUTH AFRICA—A scientist may have found the site of the "dinosaur killer"—an asteroid that, in theory, collided with Earth 65 million years ago, spewing clouds of dust that blocked the sun and caused mass extinctions.

The hypothesis was first put forward in 1979 to account for surprisingly high levels of iridium—a rare metal on the Earth's surface but abundant in extraterrestrial objects—in a layer of clay deposited over Earth during the dinosaurs' final days. The clay layer has remained a puzzle, however, because it contains forms of strontium and neodymium common to the

This secret message says
I THINK TED LIKES SUE.

They did this because letters were expensive to mail, but newspapers could be sent for free. At first, people tried hiding a note in the folds of a newspaper, but many of them were caught and punished. Then someone hit on the idea of making tiny marks with a pen or pin under certain words or letters in newspaper articles as a way of sending messages secretly.

You can hide your messages in a newspaper or magazine article in the same way. Cut out any article, and see if you can find all the letters or words of the message you want to send. Make sure they're in the right order! Then send the article to a friend who knows the secret. Keep your dots small enough so that anyone glancing casually at the article won't notice them.

Can you find the message hidden in the article above?

PIG LANGUAGES

Pig languages aren't actually languages; they're ways of hiding ordinary English words behind nonsense syllables so they sound foreign. Pig Latin and Pig Greek really don't have anything to do with Greek or Latin, and they certainly don't sound like pigs chatting over a nice trough of slop.

To speak Pig Latin, you take the first consonant sound of each word and put it at the end, and then add AY. The word *code,* for example, becomes *ode-cay.* "Let's go to the store" is *ets-lay oh-gay oo-tay ee-thay ore-stay.*

For a word that starts with a vowel, like *eat,* add WAY at the end: *eat-way.* If there is more than one consonant at the beginning of the word, transfer them all to the end and add AY. *Street* becomes *eet-stray,* for example.

In Pig Greek, add UB after the first consonant or consonants in the word. *Code* is pronounced *cub-ode* in Pig Greek. "Let's play chess" becomes *lub-ets pub-lay chub-ess.*

If the word has more than one syllable, you can throw the UB sound between each syllable: *Saturday* becomes *sub-at tub-ur dub-ay.* If there is no consonant at the beginning of the word, simply start the word with UB: *on* becomes *ub-on.*

Pig languages are real tongue-twisters, but with some practice, you'll soon be speaking like a native! Be careful, though. There are a lot of people who are very fluent in pig. Kids have been driving their parents crazy with pig languages for so long that your parents probably spoke them when they were kids. So don't try wising off in pig—it could get you into big trouble!

7

Mind Reading Tricks

Have you ever seen a magic show in which the magician claimed to have extrasensory perception (ESP)? Maybe he was able to name a playing card picked at random by someone in the audience. "Mind reading" tricks like this one look awfully convincing, but the magician and his assistants weren't using ESP—they were using secret codes and signals.

A VERBAL CODE TRICK

You can use secret verbal codes to perform fantastic feats of mind-reading. If you and a friend memorize a list of code words that stand for the suits and values of the cards in a deck of playing cards, you'll be able to tell each other exactly which card you are holding in such a sly way that nobody will know how you did it.

Here's how it works. Have your assistant ask someone in the audience to pick a card from the deck while you aren't in the room. Your assistant should place the card facedown on a table. Then you should be called back into the room.

Announce that you haven't seen the card and you don't have any idea which card it is, which is true. Then say to your assistant: "Please pick up the card and look at it. You must concentrate very hard on the card you are holding without letting me see it. Are you concentrating?"

Your assistant will respond using one of the following code words, depending on the suit of the card:

If the suit
of the card is:
Spades
Your assistant
will say:
"YES"

If the suit
of the card is:
Clubs
Your assistant
will say:
"YEAH"

If the suit
of the card is:
Hearts
Your assistant
will say:
"UH-HUH"

If the suit
of the card is:
Diamonds
Your assistant
will:
NOD

If your assistant just nods, for example, you know that the card is a diamond. Close your eyes, rub your temples, and scrunch up your face as though you are concentrating very hard. Then say something like, "Hmmm . . . I seem to be getting a very clear picture of a diamond. Am I right?"

Now your assistant responds with a coded "yes" for the value of the card. Since there are 13 numbered and face cards in each suit, you need 13 different ways of saying "Yes." Your value code might look something like this:

"YES" =KING
"YEAH"=QUEEN
NOD=JACK
"RIGHT"=10
"YOU'RE RIGHT"=9

"THAT'S RIGHT"=8
"CORRECT"=7
"THAT'S CORRECT"=6
"GOOD"=5
"VERY GOOD"=4
"YOU GOT IT!"=3
"THAT'S IT!"=2
"AMAZING!"=ACE

(I'll bet you never realized that there were so many ways to say "yes" in English! There are even more of them—try to figure out some that are easiest for you and your assistant to remember.)

Now, when your assistant answers your question about whether you were right about the suit (which, of course, you were), he or she tells you exactly which card was selected. You should go through more temple-rubbing, face-scrunching "concentration" before announcing that you have determined what the card is.

It takes some practice and some memorizing to do this trick convincingly, but won't your friends and family be amazed at your new powers?

A HAND SIGNAL TRICK

Hand signals are a great way to send secret messages to friends, but you can also use them to add to your bag of mind-reading tricks.

Every magician needs a good assistant, so teach one of your friends this trick. Together, the two of you can convince people that you have mysterious mind-reading powers. Of course, what you really have is a secret code.

Get a deck of playing cards. Take

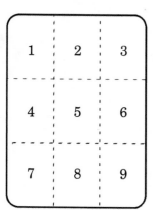

any card out and put it facedown on a table. In your imagination, divide the card into nine parts, as in the figure to the left. These nine parts are your secret key. Now deal out nine other cards facedown on the table in a 3 by 3 pattern, like this:

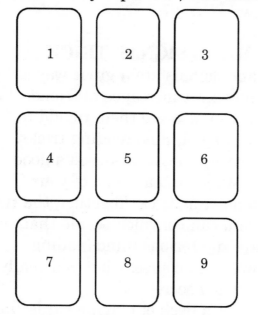

See how the nine cards are arranged like a larger version of the nine imaginary parts of the one card? By pointing to one of the nine spaces on the back of the one card, you can "tell" your assistant which of the nine cards you want to have turned over. Practice doing this on the one card while your assistant turns over the corresponding target card in the group of nine. For example, if you touch the card here:

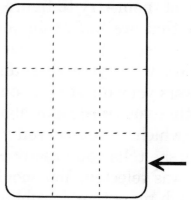

you're telling your partner to turn over the card in position number 9. If you touch the card smack in the middle, you want your assistant to turn over the middle card (the card in position number 5).

Now you're ready to demonstrate to an audience how you and your friend have ESP. Deal any nine cards, facedown, in the 3 by 3 pattern. Send your assistant out of the room. Ask someone in the audience to turn over any one card. Show this card to everyone, then replace it in the 3 by 3 pattern—but remember where it is! Then call your assistant back in.

Say to your assistant, "I am concentrating on the card that someone in our audience turned over. We all know which one it is, but you don't. I'll send you a picture of it in my mind, and then you'll be able to tell me which card it is."

After "concentrating" awhile, touch one of the nine cards—not the target card—on the spot showing the real location of the target card. Ask, "Is this the right card?"

Your assistant, who now knows the location of the target card, will say, "No, that's not it." Point to other cards and ask the same question, but don't use the code again, or someone might catch on.

When you touch the right card, your assistant should say, "Yes, that's the one, I can feel it very strongly." Your audience will be amazed.

Riddles to Solve

1 What did one mouse have to give her friend who fell into the river? (Use the shift cipher on page 27.)

PRXVH–WR–PRXVH
UHVXVFLWDWLRQ

2 What can be measured but has no length, width or thickness? (Use the Polybius number cipher on page 26.)

45 15 33 41 15 43 11 45 51 43 15

3 How can you eat an egg without cracking it? (Use the random symbol cipher on page 32.)

↑○☆⚹ ◐△↓◓△▽◎ ◒⊠◎◎
●Ƨ○●⊙ ↔→

4 Why do mother kangaroos hate rainy days? (Use the key word column cipher on page 25 with key word *cipher*.)

BEDTI UKVAD AEALI ETSON CHHPS SIEYE

5 What's the hardest thing about learning to ice skate? (Use Braille, page 30.)

• • • • • • • •
• • • • • • •
•

6 Two boys were born on the exact same day at the same place to the same parents, but they aren't twins. How can this be? (Use the up-and-down cipher on page 21.)

TEWR TOF HE TILT HYE EWOT RERPES.

7 What can you hold in your right hand but not in your left hand? (Use the telephone dial machine code on page 36.)

9• 6• 8̇ 7   5• 3̇ 3• •8   3̇ 5• 2̇ 6• •9

8 If you threw a yellow stone into the Red Sea, what would it become? (Use Morse code on page 46.)

. _ _ / . / _

9 What kind of animal doesn't play fair? (Use the random substitution cipher with typewriter symbols on page 32.)

! *?×× =!?

10 What does a pig write with? (Use the pigpen cipher on page 28.)

11 What's as big as an elephant but doesn't weigh anything? (Use Polybius cipher on page 26.)

11 34   15 32 15 41 23 11 34 45 44   44 23 11 14 35 53

12 What should you know before trying to teach a dog tricks? (Use the pigpen cipher on page 28.)

13 What kinds of buildings are the tallest? (Use the shift cipher on page 27.)

OLEUDULHV–WKHB KDYH WKH PRVW VWRULHV

14 What is the beginning of eternity, The end of time and space, The beginning of every end, And the end of every race? (Use the telephone dial code machine on page 36.)

·8 4 3̇   5· 3̇ ·8 ·8 3̇ 7̇   3̇

15 What coded message is the same from left to right, right to left, upside down and right side up? (Use the manual alphabet on page 50.)

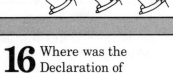

16 Where was the Declaration of Independence signed? (Use Morse code, found on page 46.)

. _ / _ // _ / . . . . / . / _ . . . /
_ _ _ / _ / _ / _ _ _ / _ _

17 What is brought to the table and cut but not eaten? (Use the key word column cipher on page 25; the key word is SLOP.)

DOR EFD CCS AKA

18 What kind of mouse can jump higher than a house? (Use the random symbol cipher on page 32.)

▽○▽◁ ○+▽○ ≠ ○ ↑△△◎◎
●○△→ ◊△↑∽

19 Why does a dog scratch himself? (Use a 6×6 winding way cipher in this pattern:)

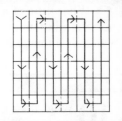

BEE ORCH EWL NECOSSIE
ST WEO AUNK HIX QT ENES

20 How do you keep from getting a sharp pain in your eye when quickly drinking a cold glass of chocolate milk? (Use a 5×5 winding way cipher with this pattern:)

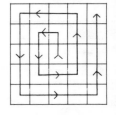

OSEN FTHUP EKATH OOG LASSE TOT

ANSWERS:

1. Mouse-to-mouse resuscitation.
2. Temperature.
3. Have someone else crack it.
4. Because the kids have to play inside.
5. The ice.
6. They were two of three triplets.
7. Your left elbow.
8. Wet.
9. A cheetah.
10. A pigpen.
11. An elephant's shadow.
12. More than the dog.
13. Libraries—they have the most stories.
14. The letter E.
15. SOS.
16. At the bottom.
17. A deck of cards.
18. Any kind. A house can't jump.
19. Because no one else knows where it itches.
20. Take the spoon out of the glass.

Index

About the Author

Eleanor A. Grant is a freelance writer and editor who lives in Ardmore, Pennsylvania. She has written for science and medical magazines.